Double Take Marketing Techniques

Another Big Idea Marketing Strategy

by Jerry Bader

MRP

WEBMEDIA

Written & Photographed by Jerry Bader
Actress, Model, Dancer: Jennifer Thiessen

blurb

What This Book Is All About

People are inundated with commercial messages from the time they get up in the morning to the time they go to bed. It isn't just radio, television, and the Internet. It's magazines, roadside billboards, and your mobile phone; it's even crept into professional sports uniforms. Much of this advertising noise is ignored, filtered out by a market that has had enough. As a marketer you have to find ways to cut through the noise, to get people to pay attention to your message, in short, to take a second look at what you have to say.

Double-Take Marketing Techniques
Another Big Idea Strategy

How To Make Your Audience Take a Second Look

We've all seen the comic 'double take:' a kind of startled second look that was refined to perfection by old-time vaudeville comics and animators who over-emphasized the gesture to humorous effect. It's the result of experiencing something that you're not sure you actually saw, so you have to take a second look. It is something marketers should consider because getting your audience to give your presentation, ad, video, or website a second look, is just what you need them to do.

The vast majority of people think speed and brevity are the keys to customer engagement but in fact speed and brevity are engagement killers. They are as ineffective and counter-productive in marketing as they are in the bedroom. You want your audience to slow down, pay attention, absorb the material, and take a second look, because the more they pay attention, the more they'll understand your company is the one they need. This is especially true on the Internet where confidence in the company you're buying from is paramount in closing a sale. We've all experienced the glib, fast-talking salesmen, and websites that emulate that experience are quickly eliminated as potential suppliers, as are the websites that lack any discernible personality and reek of boredom.

In this Big Idea installment we'll attempt to provide you with some ideas for how to stop your audience in its tracks and get them to pay attention to what your content has to say, and entice them to learn more about what you do, and how you can help satisfy their needs and desires. There is one caveat of course, there always is, isn't there: you have to have something of substance to say, and something of value to offer.

Concept 1

Awaken Your Brand's Cognitive Itch

We've all had the experience of a song or commercial jingle that gets stuck in our heads. It's an experience James Kellaris of the University of California calls 'cognitive itch'. Kellaris points to three ingredients that produce the effect: simplicity, repetition, and incongruity. The way pop music is composed and marketed takes full advantage of all three ingredients.

If you were looking for a formula for advertising success then these three elements are probably the three that you'd need to implement. If your audience doesn't understand what you're selling, and why they should care, your chance of success is unlikely. Keep it simple stupid, or KISS, is an often-repeated aphorism, albeit a bit simplistic when you consider the third ingredient, incongruity; but before we get to it, lets take a look at repetition. The payola scandals of the 1950s were in fact a repetition marketing tactic used to prime the record sales pump by paying disc jockeys to play a particular song over and over again until it crept into the public's consciousness and sales soared.

Today, an evening in front of the television is an experience fraught with irritation perpetrated by advertisers who use the repetition tactic as if it was some kind of rendition style torture used to brainwash the public into becoming

The Tattooed Lady
Engagement Technique 1

There was a time when tattoos were reserved for drunken sailors on leave, but times have changed.

Today, tattoos are hot and what could be hotter than a beautiful woman with a beautiful tattoo. It may not be for everyone, but if cutting-edge describes your brand, it might just be a way to get people to stop and take a second look.

shopping zombies. By repeating an inane, simplistic commercial message over and over, advertisers hope to create a knee jerk purchase from the living dead who blindly stumble through suburban shopping malls buying everything that was advertised on last nights hit television show. And of course the tactic works, creating a massive barrier of advertising noise that is literally impossible for the small and medium size business to break through.

The Internet was initially a communication venue where small and medium-sized businesses could compete with big business on an equal footing. But as audience interest and participation grew, so too did big businesses' influence, by increasing their investment in controlling the opportunities available; if not in direct ownership like they've done in cable TV, then in dominating advertising space. A scenario that plays into the hands of the ad-tech superpowers who have been drawn into Wall Street's avaricious orbit, driving up advertising costs, thereby limiting the ability of SMEs to compete or be heard amongst the flood of big budget advertising noise.

Which brings us to the ingredient that provides the most promise for online entrepreneurs. When the dumb-and-dumber simplicity and repetition of the corporate approach limits your ability to be heard, you have to try something different, and that something different is incongruity.

Incongruity, The Cognitive Key

I'm not suggesting that online entrepreneurs should ignore the notions of simplicity and repetition, but rather, incorporate them into an incongruity strategy. Where big business uses a scorched-earth advertising policy using every communication venue available to fill the broadcast airwaves and narrowcast net-waves with continuous gibber-jabber, the small guy must use a more narrowly focused strategic approach to reach his or her audience: an approach that uses a take-a-second-look tactic designed to penetrate the noise and slow the audience down so that the message gets seeded in the audience's subconscious. Incongruity forces the audience to think in order to solve the puzzle. By forcing your audience to work out the incongruity you create memory, and if your audience doesn't remember your brand, you're not going to sell them.

Incongruity-Resolution Theory

I-R Theory, or Incongruity-Resolution Theory, states that the humor that produces laughter and memory results from the 'aha moment' formed by the brain's resolution of the incongruities created through the process of setup, elaboration, twist, and resolution.

Because we are hardwired to look for patterns of behavior in order to make quick decisive decisions, a survival mechanism, we often make false assumptions. Humor, drama, storytelling, and creativity in general are all based on the tension created by building assumption-filled scenarios allowing the audience to resolve the conflicts between those assumptions and reality; thereby releasing the tension and providing a feeling of accomplishment and success. The reaction to solving a riddle creates a powerful memory that in business terms is the goal of all marketing communication. And perhaps just as importantly, the resolution of incongruities produces a kind of link or bond between the viewer and advertiser, a shared "I get it" moment that creates a quasi-social glue.

The Caricature Effect
Engagement Technique 2

What we notice is what's different; it's how we recognize faces and distinguish friends from foes. It's hardwired into our brains as a survival mechanism; and it's the reason why caricature artists have been around since man was able to pickup a pencil and draw.

When a phenomenon is so vital to our very being why not use it as a way to get your audience to take a second look.

Concept 2

Ooey-Gooey Stickiness

The ability to be noticed and remembered is becoming increasingly difficult in a marketplace inundated and overwhelmed by ever-increasing content, deafening advertising noise, and countless competitive and repetitive options. Stickiness is of course the quality of your content to retain your audience long enough to receive your message. Attracting large numbers of visitors who instantly opt-out because they were misled to your website, or who find nothing relevant to their needs, does not advance your marketing objectives. Even worse, real potential customers can be scared away if you fail to engage their minds in some meaningful manner, because if you can't engage their minds, you'll never access their wallets.

By slowing your audience down so they pay attention to your message, you automatically create "stickiness:" the ability to hold an audience's attention long enough to intrigue them to find out more, and get them physically and cognitively involved in discovering who your brand is, what your brand does, and why they should care. If you can get your audience to stick around long enough to convey these three messages you have a good chance of being remembered, and maybe have them pick up the phone or email.

To be sticky you have to be special; you have to standout; you have to be bold; and unafraid to make a distinctive statement, with the understanding that some people will love what you do and how you do it, and others won't. Why waste time with tire-kickers that are never going to buy from you anyway? By making a definitive statement you qualify your audience. And the sticky concept doesn't just apply to websites: display ads in magazines or retail window posters can become instantly sticky by adding interactive elements like QR Codes and Augmented Reality videos, accessed with the click of a smart phone button.

Advertising is meant to make you stop and think and cognitively engage you, so the brand story gets ingrained in the deepest recesses of your audience's mind. The consistent delivery of a core brand story moves the mental process from episodic to semantic memory, thereby incorporating the message into the audience's core belief system; let your competition compete with that.

Concept 3

Rethink Your Approach

Sometimes a simple change in approach can make all the difference in the world. Instead of thinking of your website as a brochure, or an exercise in search engine optimization, social media or e-commerce; instead of thinking of your next advertising campaign as an exercise in hyping your latest feature upgrade; start thinking of all your marketing materials from websites to business cards as a chance to tell your brand story.

It's your opportunity to communicate with your audience 'mano a mano'. But you can't communicate if don't slow them down long enough to pay attention to what you have to say. And of course, you have to make sure what you have to say is worth listening to, or you'll likely never have another chance to say anything.

Get Uptight
Engagement Technique 3

Get in close and focus on making
eye contact. Get rid of all the
extraneous elements that distract
attention and get in the way.
Studies show that making eye
connect increases audience
engagement.

So what's important? If you've read any of the previous installments of the Big Idea series you'll know that Maslow's Hierarchy of Needs is the place to find the key to your audience's hearts and minds. Maslow provides the combination needed to unlock your audience's pocketbooks. E-commerce sites that present someone else's branded merchandise are merely a commodity play that only benefits the lowest price seller. Sites that offer everything and anything only serve to confuse and frustrate an audience with a paradox of choice. Feature-bloat and benefit-hyperbole are just as ineffective, as is an uptight pseudo-corporate façade in an effort not to offend anyone and appear substantial, like an insurance company, or some other soulless bureaucratic black-hole of service. Find the psychological and emotional need hardwired deep in your audience's psyche, and you'll make the connection that leads to a sale.

Concept 4

Stories Put Information Into Context

Stories are the glue that provides people with the ability to retain information because the message is placed inside some meaningful context. We read our children Aesop's fables not just to get them to go to sleep but to ingrain in them some sense of morality and justice, the sort of moral suasion that makes for a pretty good advertising model.

Politicians are the quintessential salesmen; they understand that the average voter is not going to follow a fact-filled justification for a program initiative, so instead they tell stories: health care policies are explained by illustrating how little Johnny, from Springfield, MA is going to be able to get his new heart, and that his mother will not have to work in the all-night laundry in horrendous heat and humidity to pay for the operation, all because of this politician's new bill.

Stories are patterns of information constructed with a beginning, middle, and an end; and a good story, well delivered, provides the emotional satisfaction that fires the endorphins that make the message memorable and actionable.

Concept 5

Focus On A Single Message

Mixed and confusing messages are the death knell of any advertising, whether it's a Web-video or print ad campaign. No matter how much you want to cram every idea, concept, feature, or benefit into a presentation, resist. The difference between memorable and forgettable is your ability to discipline yourself to focus attention on the one thing that will capture people's imagination.

Everyone uses the Internet as a communication venue, but very few people understand the implications of how they are communicating, or what makes the Internet such a powerful environment. The multimedia nature of the Internet allows the use of sights, sounds, and text in order to convey meaning, but few people understand the cognitive impact of images, sounds, and even words.

The proper implementation of multimedia focuses attention and helps deliver impact, turning content into meaning.

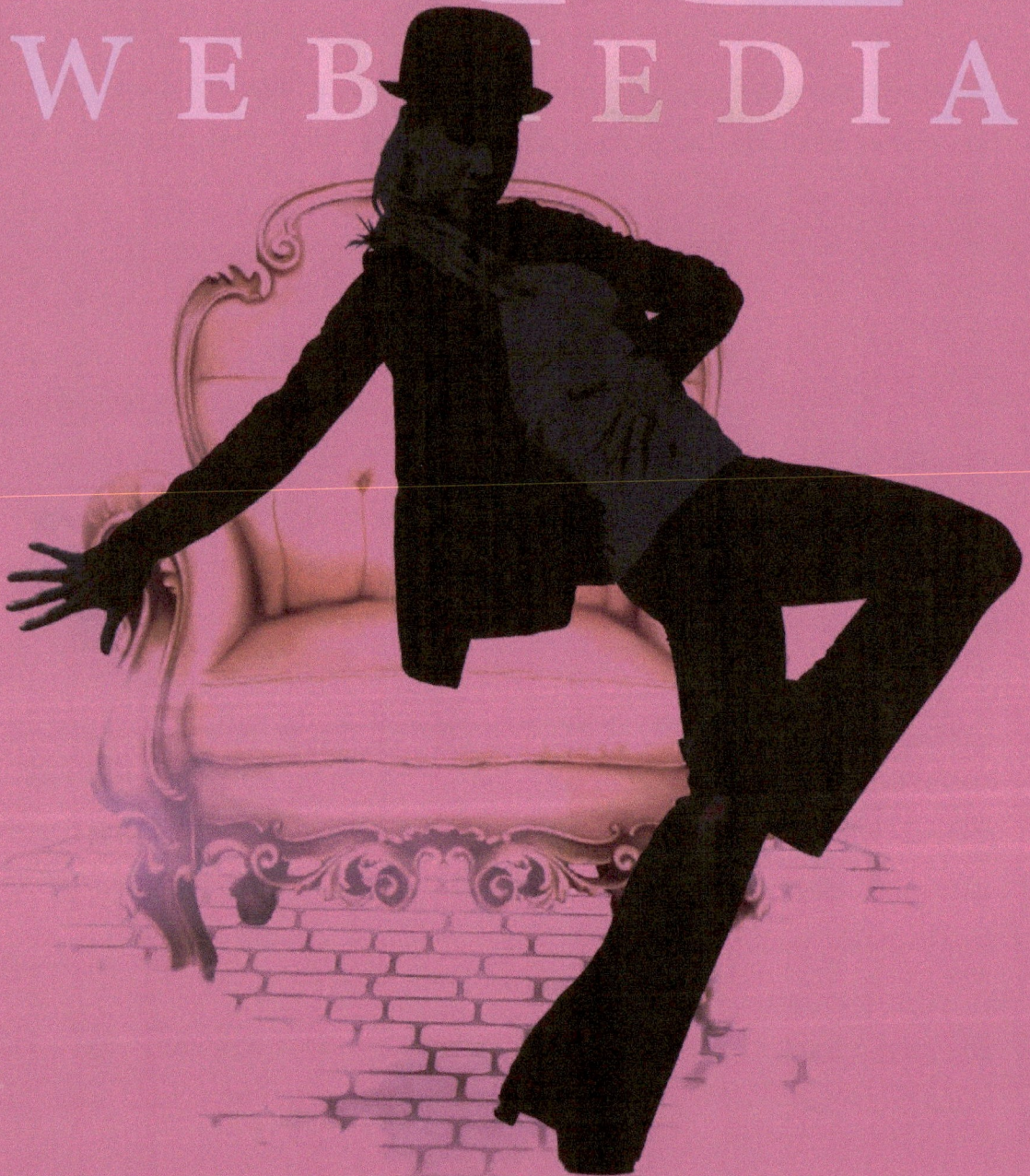

Slipstream Away
Engagement Technique 4

Remember those original Apple iPod ads with the almost silhouette dancer grooving to the latest hit over a brightly colored background. Certain images and scenes are classic and by slipstreaming their essence you can grab an audience's attention and get them to take a second look.

Concept 6

Give Your Presentation A Twist

Jokes, magic, stories, and effective commercial advertisements all have one thing in common, they need to draw an audience in with the familiar, enhance the scenario with detail and elaboration, and end with a twist. The approach is unlimited in that it can be used in print and multimedia. All effective marketing needs a punch-line: some kind of clever twist, something to excite the brain and force it to do some work and unravel the conundrum, even if its purpose is as mundane as which laundry detergent to buy, or which supplier to choose.

"Whenever I meet a pretty girl, the first thing I look for is intelligence; because if she doesn't have it, she's mine."

"I once went on a date with a girl where we went hiking, and she gets bit by a snake in-between her toes, and I had to suck out the poison… so she's dead."
- Comedian Anthony Jeselnik

Concept 7

Sights and Sounds Trigger Emotion and Memory

Whether you're writing copy for your website or a script for your video, your words need to deliver the sights and sounds that trigger memories. It's those recalled experiences that will be associated with your presentation and make it memorable. This is not an off-the-shelf stock approach. To use a photograph, music theme, or video sequence that has been used by hundreds of other companies for a variety of goods and services is pointless at best and counter-productive at worst. If you're afraid to make a statement, nobody will pay any attention to you. And you don't have to shout at people like the late Billy Mays' just to get an audience's attention.

QR Codes and Augmented Reality allow sights and sounds to be incorporated into almost any communication vehicle. The sound of hot coffee being poured into a mug on a Web-ad evokes the smell of your favorite brand during a relaxing Sunday morning brunch. A newspaper or magazine print ad that springs to life with an augmented reality video generates awareness and desire in the viewer. Sights and sounds trigger the memory that associates your brand with the emotional triggers that drive action.

Concept 8

Rhyme, Rhythm and Repetition: A Pattern of Pleasure

Whether it's the recipe for a Big Mac or the script for the haunting Lexus 'Moments' voice-over, the influence of rhyme, rhythm, and repetition cannot be underestimated. The creation of an emotional, auditory, sensory experience provides the cognitive impact that all consummate marketing professionals aim to achieve.

We are emotional creatures. We crave patterns, order, and metaphorical mnemonic reference in order to make sense out of our experiences. The original

Get A Concept
Engagement Technique 5

The mind is constantly scanning for puzzles, problems, and conundrums to solve; it's just how we're wired.

So why not create a puzzle, an incongruity that demands your audience take a second look. It doesn't have to be wild and crazy, well maybe just a little crazy, but crazy is what will make them pay attention and absorb your message.

'Moments' commercial written by Glen Hunt turned a single word into an effective campaign, based on the creative use of rhyme, rhythm and repetition. It's a technique that provides a model that can be used to make an impression and influence action. Sometimes we forget how powerful words alone can be; and that the mere act of reading them can produce a memorable experience.

Time: An Exercise in Rhyme, Rhythm, and Repetition

It's about time …
Time to live. Time to love.
Time to think. Time to learn.
There's a stitch-in-time, and the time of your life.
There's makeup-time, breakup-time, even coffee-time.
There's half-time, full-time, and part-time …
And of course, the all-important, time-and-a-half.

You can have time …
You can run-out of time, or you can be in-time.
You can be on time, or you can tell the time.
There's also a time and a place …
You can have plenty of time, or you can give someone your time.
You can have time on your hands.
But there's no time like the present …

You know that time waits for no man,
And inevitably, time marches on.
There are good-times and bad-times.
There's even Doing Time.
There's time well spent or just wasting time.
Things can be well-timed, timeless, timely, or even 'of -a-time' …
But in the end … Time's Up.
So Stop Wasting Time!

Concept 9

Credibility: Keep It Real, Be Believable

If there is one thing that every Web-company needs to establish it's credibility. No matter how much traffic you generate with false promises, contrived promotions, or outlandish claims, it will all lead to naught, if you've failed to build trust and believability.

We spend a lot of time and effort in providing our audience with interesting material, most of which asks for nothing in return. We always provide a phone number and contact name for any advertising, promotion, or website that we develop. We always answer emails and attempt to be helpful to inquiries even when we know nothing in the way of business will come of it.

Our philosophy is simple, we offer our audience marketing advise and creative services based on our experience, our unique point-of-view, and an unusual set of skills and expertise. It's our way of creating credibility. Can you say the same?

Concept 10

Emotion: Elicit An Emotional Experience

Emotion has always got a bad rap when it comes to business. The nation's business schools have perpetuated the myth of business as science with charts, spreadsheets, and statistical analysis. The technical fascination associated with the Internet has continued this fairy tale, but the fact is business, or at least the

"Sure, I bet!"

"Not now!"

"It was how big?"

"Get a life!"

"Same to you."

"Your place, or mine?"

"Ya, sure."

"Yikes!"

"That was fun."

The Mirroring Effect
Engagement Technique 6

Psychologists have observed an
emotional mirroring effect in people
when they experience highly
charged emotional experiences.

An image that displays a genuine
emotional reaction can access
feelings in your audience that
demand they take a second look.
And if an image can achieve
mirroring, imagine what a video
can achieve when done right.

sales and marketing function, is all about eliciting emotional response through the implementation of psychological strategies in creative presentation.

The entertainment business is a prime example of how bean counters can destroy any business. Nobody really knows specifically why some movies and some songs are hits and others are failures. We can identify certain elements that factor into success, but removed from the totality of a specific presentation these singular elements become meaningless. It's the synchronicity of the combination of elements that counts, the way they work together as a whole that makes the magic – the whole is greater than the sum of the parts.

There is no tried and true formula that producers can follow to guarantee a success; that is unless they can tap into the emotional needs of the audience. Find the emotional need in your audience and build a Web-marketing campaign around that need.

Concept 11

How Sound Design Affects Customer Response And Action

If you've spent a small fortune on graphic designers, search engine optimizers, social networking experts and you still find that your website conversions are low, then perhaps your website suffers from the marketing equivalent of Capgras Delusion, a failure to make a connection between your online content and your audience's emotional core.

The ability to tap into an audience's emotions is the key to converting interested visitors into paying customers and long-term clients. Marketing and advertising executives have experimented with all kinds of subliminal and psychological techniques over the years, but the most powerful and obvious technique has been staring them right in the face, or more precisely, reverberating in their ears.

You're Not My Wife

A woman phones her husband who's in the hospital after suffering a head injury. The man recognizes his wife's voice when she tells him she'll see him in an hour. An hour later she arrives at the hospital, enters the room, and attempts to kiss him on the forehead. The man looks up at his wife startled, and says, "Who the hell are you?"

The man recognizes the woman in front of him as someone who looks like his wife, but he is completely convinced that she is an imposter even though he recognized his wife's voice over the phone only an hour earlier. This is a classic case of Capgras Delusion. The part of the brain responsible for visual recognition is functioning fine, but the part that makes the connection between his wife's appearance and what she means to him emotionally has been severed.

Without An Emotional Connection Marketing Appears Fake

The brain is made-up of various systems that operate both separately and in unison with each other. The brain's interpretive emotional mechanism, the Limbic System, is what gives meaning to the objects, images, sounds and the people we encounter.

ReelHeadShots

The video above is part of our ReelHeadShot service for actors, models, and entertainers. Along with the video audition we create a series of headshots like the ones seen on the Mirroring Effect page that display an actors ability to perform and connect to an audience on an emotional level. If you've purchased the print edition you can access the video on our YouTube channel (http://youtu.be/D-gT-WPhBLw).

Tell A Story
Engagement Technique 7

There's a reason politicians' always explain their policies by relating them to an ordinary citizen rather than explaining the macro effects that may benefit society as a whole. People relate to stories, they humanize issues and clarify problems that may otherwise seem remote and irrelevant. Stories are how we learn, how we understand, and how we relate. If your brand doesn't tell a story, it will not get people to take a second look.

Exaggerate
Engagement Technique 8

One way to cut through the advertising noise is to push the visual limits, to exaggerate so your point is clear and concise.

Subtlety can be lost on a distracted and perpetually busy target audience trying to do too many things at once; and therefore, not in any condition to hear or understand your message.

We take the ordinary for granted because ordinary carries no weight; it is neither interesting nor exciting. Ordinary is just the same-old-same-old, and in advertising, that just won't cut it. Exaggeration may just be the tactic that gets your audience to take a second look; so stretch the limbs, push the pose, or do whatever needs to be done to get your audience to do a double take.

Without this emotional connection things have no meaning and, in fact, can be regarded as fake. Observations of Capgras Delusional patients illustrate how fundamental the sense of sound is in giving meaning to the world around us. Sound, it appears, is an even more important sense than sight in terms of attaching meaning to what we experience, a fact website owners and marketing executives need to consider when developing a Web video presentation, or in any brand imaging effort.

Sound: The Final Frontier
Sound is fundamental to our survival as a species and our functioning as successful communal creatures both in our private and business lives. Sound is one of the most complex and least understood tools marketing people have, but at the same time it is probably the most important, especially when associated with video imaging.

Julian Treasure, sound expert, tells us that sound affects an audience in four fundamental ways: physiologically, psychologically, cognitively and behaviorally. Sounds paint emotionally charged mental images even without the aid of visual stimuli. The sound of a crackling fire, coffee percolating, a baby crying, or a woman screaming evokes vivid images and associations in our heads and fills us with emotional responses. The sound of thunder sends us scrambling for cover.

The rhythmic beat of a favorite song gets our toes tapping and our heads bopping. The sound of a catchy fast food jingle gets our mouths watering, creating an instant craving for a hamburger and fries. The rhythmic recital of the alphabet helps children remember their ABCs. And so on.

Sound can get your heart racing with excitement or slow it down to a state of mellow meditation. Sound can remind you of things you love, releasing endorphins and a desire to pursue the object of attraction. Sound can inform, enlighten and educate. Use sound wisely in your Web video or in your place of business, and it will communicate, influence and persuade; use it poorly and it will send your potential customers racing for the exits or your competitor's website, without a second's hesitation.

Sound Tools

We associate sound with entertainment, but for marketers it is a tool to be used to convert prospects into clients. When someone comes to your website they are for at least a moment, a captive attentive audience. If your goal is to maximize impact you must use all the tools available, and that means sight and sound.

Voice

The sound of the human voice is the most powerful sound tool marketers have at their disposal. The ability to control tonal quality, pitch, cadence and phrasing is unsurpassed as a means of delivering a meaningful, memorable marketing communication. Sound is the foundation of experience and nothing is as capable of infinite variation, nuance and meaning as the human voice.

If you pay attention to television commercials you will recognize many signature voices associated with brands: Sam Elliot, Keifer Sutherland, John O'Hurley, and the list goes on. Those old enough to remember the original 7-Up Uncola

Emotional Expression
Engagement Technique 9

There is a reason that actors are actors and business executives are business executives. You have to resist the current ego trend to want to be a star. Just because the Internet provides a venue that gives you the opportunity to present yourself doesn't mean you're the right person to deliver your message.

Actors are trained to use their voices and deliver dialogue that resonates with an audience, and they know how to use body language and most importantly facial expression in order to connect to viewers.

If you want your message to penetrate the consciousness of your target market you need to deliver genuine emotional expression. Bland faces and phony smiles aren't going to get your viewers to take a second look.

commercials of the 1970s will remember the distinctive sound of Geoffrey Holder, or the unique clipped phrasing and cadence of Rod Serling's late 1950s 'Twilight Zone' introductions.

Would people still remember classic television shows like the original 'The Prisoner' or 'Dragnet' without the sounds of Patrick McGoohan and Jack Webb ringing in their ears? Remakes and sequels just don't work without the power, presence and impact of those original distinctive voices.

Music

Music has always been a central and significant part of people's lives. You need think no further than the notion of "our song" a musical representation of how two people feel about each other. Every generation has their sound, their musical heroes, and a play-list of their lives. The smart brands know how to use music to create emotional context and memorable experiences. There is no reason smaller companies can't do the same thing.

In an effort to promote radio advertising, Bob McCurdy created a website presentation 'The Power of Sound' to introduce people to some of the fundamental influences of sound in a commercial context. In his presentation McCurdy mentions numerous examples, including an article by Adrian C. North, David J. Hargreaves and Jennifer McKendrick that were featured in the 'Journal of Applied Psychology.' The example describes how sound can influence prospective customers. French and German music were played on alternate days promoting in-store wine displays. Sales of French wines outsold German wines on the days that French music was played, and the reverse was true on days when the German music was played. In another example McCurdy refers to an article by Adrian C. North, Amber Shilcock and David J Hargreaves as reported in 'Environment and Behavior.' It details how classical music played in a British restaurant led to higher per table spending by customers as compared to the days when pop or no music was played.

Rhythm

No truer words have been spoken, or in this case sung, than when Gloria Estefan sang 'The Rhythm Is Going To Get You'. Concert crowds move in synchronized response to the rhythm of the performance as if controlled by some brainwave entrainment, a phenomenon that describes the brain's ability to synchronize it's own electrical cycles to external rhythmic sensory stimulation.

Entrainment is a normal occurrence in nature and was first discovered in 1656 by Christian Huygens, who found that the pendulums in a room full of grandfather clocks all synchronize themselves to the same rhythm even when they initially all started swinging at different rates. In his paper 'On the Effects of Lullabies', Johannes Kneutgen describes how a baby's breathing, rhythmically responds to music. Since brain waves pulsate like sound waves in cycles per second, it is easy to see how the phenomenon of entrainment can have a fundamental effect on how we think and react to rhythmic stimulation.

Context

In Bob McCurdy's presentation 'The Power of Sound' he describes how in the 1970s, IBM worked to eliminate the sound of their new electric typewriters in an attempt to provide a better work environment, but the effort had a negative

Focus
Engagement Technique 10

Focusing on a single high concept big idea that defines your brand is the most effective strategy for achieving the image and identity that will make you the market leader. The principle of focus not only applies to ideas it also applies to imagery and presentation. A cluttered image or presentation is as ineffective as a cluttered verbal one. Think like a director, think focus, and you'll get your audience to take a second look.

effect. IBM had to add back an electronic sound to the typewriters as typists found the silence disconcerting. The rhythmic sound gave the operators assurance that they were on-task and accomplishing something and that the typewriters were working properly.

A Nissan team of engineers led by music consultant, Toshiyuki Tabata, had to create an artificial high-pitched sound similar to the flying cars in the movie 'Blade Runner' for their new hybrids, as drivers felt the silent running hybrids were missing something. And in fact the silent automobile was a potential traffic hazard as other vehicles and pedestrians could not hear it coming. In the same regard when the Las Vegas casino, The Bellagio, tried to eliminate the irritating sound made by slot machines, slot machine revenue decreased, forcing them to put the familiar sound effects back on the machines.

We are surrounded by sounds that give us reference, warning and comfort, without which we would lose much of the contextual information we need to function effectively on a daily basis. Big business uses sound design to create differentiating mental references for their products and brands ranging from the signature sound of how different car doors shut, to the unique crunch sounds of various breakfast cereals.

Sound Effects

McCurdy cites Herb Shuldiner's report in 'Motor Matters' regarding British psychologist, David Moxon, who found the sound of a Maserati engine turned-on women more than men, even if those women had no previous interest in cars.

An observation that must not have escaped Mazda when they created their "zoom, zoom" campaign. Perhaps any guy who wants to dump the suburban van for something with a bit more zip should take his wife to a Maserati dealership.

People react to sound instinctively, a phenomenon referred to as an 'orienting reflex' first described by Ivan Sechenov, a Russian physiologist, in his 1863 book 'Reflexes of the Brain' and later referred to by Ivan Pavlov, famous for his stimulus-response work with dogs, as the "What is it?" reflex. Sound effects are the mnemonics of our lives; they attract attention, they generate interest, they stimulate emotion, and they create desire.

The power of sound is an essential tool in a marketer's effort to communicate, influence and persuade an audience, and isn't that what your marketing is suppose to do?

Concept 12

Everything Matters

'Wired' magazine published an intriguing article entitled 'Very Short Stories' where they asked a number of authors to create a story in only six words. At first this seems to be an impossible task, but as you'll see it's an excellent example of how our brains form patterns out of incomplete information.

One of the best 'Very Short Stories' was by Canadian novelist, Margaret Atwood, "Corpse parts missing. Doctor buys yacht." This macabre six-word tale tells us a

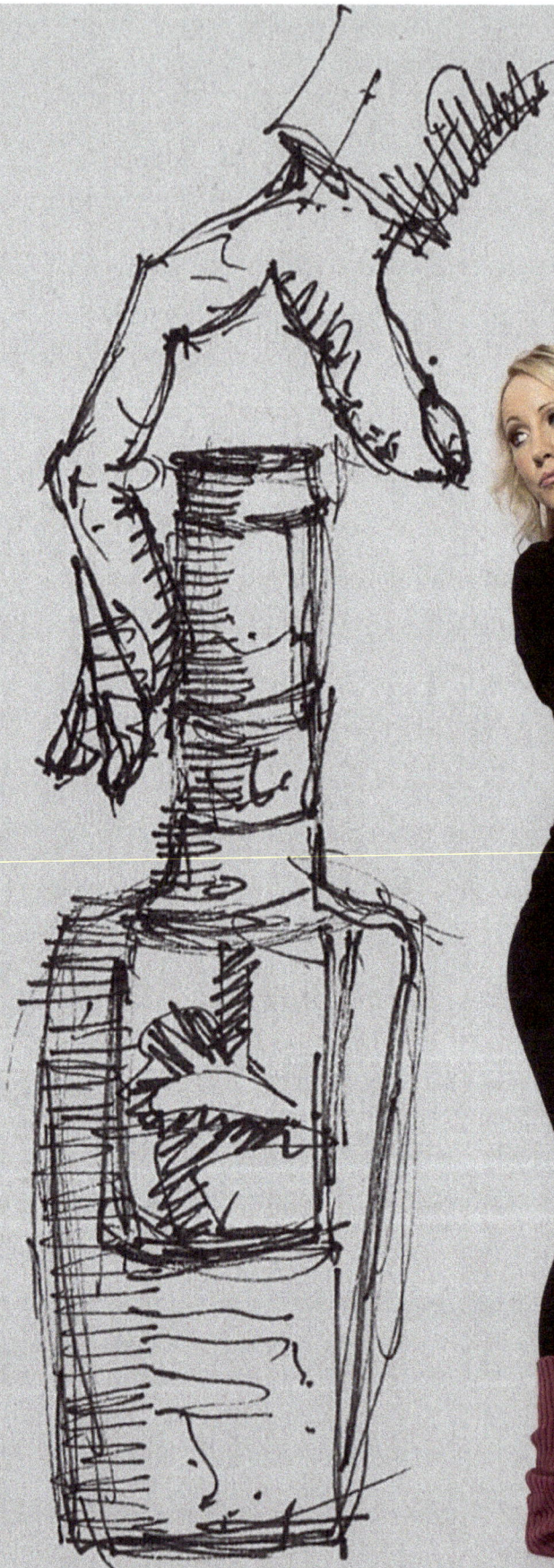

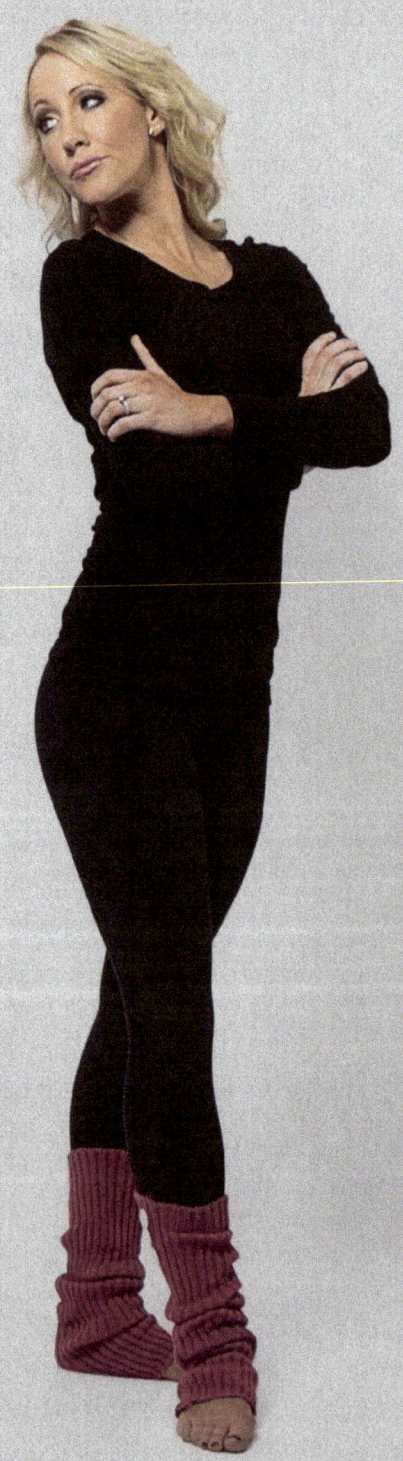

Illustrated Image
Engagement Technique 11

Combining two elements that don't belong; are rarely used together; or that present an incongruity forces the brain to solve the inconsistency. Merging a drawing and a photo into a visual story demands the viewer stop and decode the message. And if you can add a little intrigue or uncertainty, all-the-better. It may only cause a split-second's hesitation, but that may be all it takes to engage your audience and demand they take a second look.

complete story. We need no further details or explanation to understand exactly what has happened. This is an example of what the Gestaltists call 'closure' the ability of the brain to fill in the blanks in order to complete a picture or in this case to tell a story.

Cautionary Note: The example above is given as a demonstration of how powerful our brains are at forming patterns out of incomplete information. To some this may be mistaken as an endorsement of the profound idiocy of the 140-character mindset – it is not. In business it is paramount that you deliver a coherent articulate message, whether it's a text message, email, or whatever else passes for communication these days.

Margaret Atwood is an experienced award winning wordsmith, something most business people are not. Ms. Atwood's clever six-word story is an exercise in cleverness and creativity that can be misconstrued by those who mistake brevity with efficiency and glibness for clarity.

The point is words have meaning, and how you use them will be interpreted by your audience who will do so by ascribing meaning filtered through their experience, prejudice, and preconception. In short, you can use the theories of Gestalt as a weapon to win the marketing communication battle, or to inadvertently cause a self-inflicted wound that cripples your efforts.

The Whole Is Greater Than The Sum Of Its Parts

Since the early days of the Gestalt movement visual artists have had an affinity for the psychological implications of the theory. We are all familiar with Op Art's visual tricks and with Rorschach images and how we interpret them, but as you can see from Atwood's clever six-word story, this principle also works on a literary level.

Although proponents of Gestalt have been mainly concerned with the visual implications of the theory's principles, these same principles can be applied to more sophisticated problem-solving issues. The ability to form almost instantaneous conclusions from relatively little information as discussed in Malcolm Gladwell's book 'Blink' could easily be attributed to Gestalt theory.

These examples illustrate how the human brain puts pieces of information together until it recognizes a pattern that has some meaning, but is it the meaning you intended to deliver? Gestalt theory can prove to be a powerful marketing methodology if used purposefully, but it can also backfire in the hands of unsophisticated, inarticulate, intellectually immature technicians.

This phenomenon has often been boiled down to the familiar phrase: the whole is greater than the sum of its parts. When marketing disappoints, the cause most likely starts with a failure to recognize that what it's really all about is communication, and communication is as much a psychological design problem as it is an artistic or programming exercise.

The Significance of Pattern Recognition

Direct marketers have successfully used the human need for resolution, to fill-in the blanks, to sell all kinds of products. A common approach is to offer a reduced price starter kit for some collectible item like a spoon, dish, or coin that includes

Kinetic Movement
Engagement Technique 12

Kinetic movement can convey interest, excitement, and drama, even in a still image. In order to get people to stop and look, you have to provide their brains with a mental payoff, and a reason to devote some time to decoding the image and the story it tells. Kinetic movement demands resolution: what's happening, and what's going to happen next? The unresolved action demands attention, and that is all you may need to get your audience to take a second look.

the first item of a series and a display case with room for several more products. When customers get the first collectible and place it on the display provided, the empty spaces cry-out to be filled. It's an old marketing gambit, but one that works because human beings are hardwired to fill-in the blanks and complete the display or pattern.

The visual Gestalt designer will use five pattern-producing contextual techniques in order to provide the viewer with clues for completing the pattern that in-turn communicates a message.

1. **Closure:** the mind is predisposed to complete a pattern by filling in the blanks from the available information.

2. **Continuance:** the mind will follow a path seeking a conclusion or resolution from clues that point in a particular direction.

3. **Similarity:** the mind fights abstraction by trying to put the pieces of a puzzle together in some familiar form.

4. **Proximity:** the mind draws conclusions from the physical relationship of clues that clarify associations that help make the unknown known.

5. **Alignment:** the mind demands organization and will use association to create meaningful groups of information.

The Relationship of Gestalt And Brand Story Telling

Successful marketers don't need to provide every detail of a marketing message in order to deliver a meaningful presentation, in fact too much information can actually get in the way of delivering an articulate communication. Like Margaret Atwood's six-word story, meaning can be both concise and precise when the right combination of information is presented.

The difference between art for art's sake and creativity for commercial purpose is simple: once an artist finishes his or her work it then belongs to the audience who is free to interpret its meaning based on individual preconception and experience, whereas commercial creativity needs to be purposefully designed to elicit a particular response from a targeted audience. A brand story is nothing more than a pattern of psychologically manipulated information with a beginning, middle, and end. When your brain has to do a little work to put the pieces of information together to form a complete comprehensible message, that story becomes more memorable and that is exactly what marketers and advertisers strive to achieve. If we want to maximize sales we have to look at the big picture. What do we want from our audience beyond a one-shot sale of a product or service? The answer lies in how we learn, how we come to conclusions, and how we develop our personal belief systems. Our belief systems range from our political affiliation to the brand of cereal we buy.

Developing A Marketing Belief System

All marketers have learned Reis and Trout's axiom that a brand is the ownership of a piece of your audience's mind, the problem has always been how to actually acquire that valuable piece of real estate.

Perspective
Engagement Technique 13

Change the viewer's perspective;
it's a simple idea, but one that can
work to your advantage. Whether
it's a still image or video, changing
the angle of view can add interest
and drama. If you want to learn
how to add drama to your
marketing collaterals, you might
want to study the artwork in
graphic novels. The comic book
artist is a master of using
perspective to create movement and
excitement, and that's a proven
method of getting an audience to
take a second look.

The management of a business is an all consuming process that leaves little time for contemplation of conceptual problem-solving issues, but if we step back for just one moment and think of our customers as human beings, a species with the need to resolve problems and form conclusions based on a unique mental process, then maybe we can present our marketing case with more long term impact.

Everything we believe in is based on a four-part mental process that is best executed by means of a linear narrative – a compelling well-formed story.

Retention: the message we deliver must be retained in order for it to have any long-term affect.

Comprehension: the message must be understood in order for it to achieve the desired goal.

Interpretation: a well-formed message will be processed by the audience who will draw it's own conclusions based on previous knowledge or pre-existing belief systems.

Cognitive extension: once a message has been retained, understood, and interpreted, the mind will file it away and use it as a way to filter future information that relates to it.

Implications of Gestalt To An Evolving Web Environment

The principles of Gestalt and the need for human beings to resolve problems through pattern recognition have greater implications than just visual design.

As early as 1890 Austrian philosopher, Christian von Ehrenfels wrote an article, "On Gestalt Qualities' in which he pointed out that a piece of music could be recognized even when it was played in different keys where all the notes were different. The inference is clear: the need to resolve ambiguity and to solve problems is fundamental to how we think, and applies to how we process signals to our brains from all our senses, not just the visual ones.

As Internet communication slowly evolves from the presentation of mere text and static images to a richer more eloquent environment, the sophisticated marketer will need to incorporate the principles of Gestalt to better deliver their brand story – a story best told by tapping into as many senses as the environment will allow.

The power of this approach lies in it's ability to influence an audience's belief system by establishing a set of mental patterns that help your targeted audience resolve purchasing dilemmas in your favor, and at the same time, act as a barrier to competitors' less sophisticated marketing approaches.

Augmented Reality
Engagement Technique 14

Marketing is complicated; it's not just a
question of what you say; it's a question
of where you say it. Print, radio, and TV
no longer dominate; today we have
Internet ads, company websites, mobile
phones, and the ever-present social
media cesspit. What is clear is, whatever
the venue, multimedia delivery is the
way to get people to take a second look.
Companies like Layar offer a way to turn
limited-time print ads or posters into
multimedia presentations delivered on a
cell phone or iPad. And for a permanent
solution, you can use QR Codes, an
undervalued method of delivery.

Concept 13

The Caricature Effect

Marketing is all about getting noticed, getting remembered, and motivating people to action. Whether it's a website, display ad, or video, it must first grab people's attention, it must stop the viewer from going on to the next website, turning the magazine page, or clicking delete. In other words you have to stop your audience in its digital tracks and have them take a second look, but to do that you have to standout, and standing out is exactly what the Caricature Effect helps you do.

The Caricature Effect simply stated says that what we notice is variation from the norm. Caricature artists exaggerate reality because that is how we visually distinguish one person from another. Human beings are preprogrammed to look for patterns and variations in those patterns, it's how we recognize who people are, and it is a basic survival mechanism that helps us recognize danger and distinguish friend from foe.

By distorting an individual's prominent facial features the caricature artist mimics the human brain's way of remembering who's who. Our brains are not cameras that take pictures and file them away for future reference.

Our memories are malleable, they change and alter over time and experience, and as a result the things we remember best are the things that stand out, things like Bob Hope's ski-jump nose or Albert Einstein's wild white hair. The reason caricatures are so effective is because they emphasize the distinguishing differences that we recognize and remember. So how do we use this fundamental, hard-wired human characteristic to further marketing agendas?

What We Notice Is Variation From The Norm

Getting noticed is job-one of any marketing vehicle, so in order to get people to stop, look, and listen we need to use all the available communication elements at our disposal.

When developing a video campaign we use concepts that demand the mental processing of information by shocking, stimulating, puzzling, or tickling the funny bone of the viewer. These techniques force the audience to think, process, and decode the message, and by generating this mental activity we embed our client's message in the audience's consciousness. Depending on the brand and/or product, implementation can range from subtle to obvious with the goal to make people sit-up and take notice by forcing them to think.

Pattern Recognition – The Same But Different

Human beings have evolved to watch for patterns and when an audience recognizes a familiar scenario they leap to a conclusion. It's a way of making quick decisive decisions that can either help or hurt communication. Properly used pattern recognition can lead your audience where you want to take them, but if the pattern is too obvious or hackneyed, it can lead to viewers dismissing your message.

Let's face-it, consumers have become increasingly jaded by too many ads that yell at them like a Billy Mays commercial, or promise improbable results like so

Selective Color
Engagement Technique 15

Selective color is another method that
can be used to focus attention on an
important aspect of your message.
Whether it's used to emphasize the
brand's signature color or the product
itself, selective color is an effective tactic
if used with intent.

There are many variations of
implementing this technique, but what's
important is whatever variation you
choose, it must be used to focus attention
with purpose if you want your audience
to take a second look.

many diet schemes, or scare the hell out of people with legal disclaimers warning of everything from headaches to heart attacks like most prescription drug ads. These feeble attempts to standout like a pair of John Daley golf slacks only succeed in reminding the audience how completely desperate, or disengaged the advertiser really is.

If you want people to remember your message you have to alter the pattern by varying from the norm so that it forces people to mentally process your information. It's as simple as a story with a twist like how a comedian sets-up a punch line, or how a magician sets-up an illusion.

I've written extensively about techniques for using video but let's discuss something even more universal, photography. It is one of the most economical ways to create the kind of mental stimulation that makes people remember your site and your message.

Concept 14

Photo-Visual Engagement Techniques

Most every website has photography of some sort on it, but like most video implementations, it is rarely used to its full potential. Obviously, do-it-yourself snapshots reek of amateurism but even professional royalty-free images can be as innocuous as DIY snaps are unprofessional, and as we have stated, bland, generic images are just not going to stimulate anyone's memory.

Cinegraphs

Cinegraphs are photographs that move; they are created by combining a series of still images into a gif animation. The best cinegraphs use subtle movement like hair or clothing blowing in the wind to cause the audience to take a second look. What appears at first to be an ordinary still photograph creates a "Did I just see it move?" reaction, and that's the kind of subtle yet powerful feature that can get people to remember your site, your product, and your brand. Like any technique you have to know how and when to use it in order to enhance your presentation and reinforce your message. Just parachuting in a technique for technique's sake is no better than a meaningless royalty free image used as filler.

Sequence Images

A sequence image is a still image that combines a series of images into one photograph. Unlike cinegraphs, the image doesn't move but it does provide a kinetic quality by showing a series of varying poses all combined into one photograph. This kind of image can be very striking and powerful and can cause your viewer to take a moment to decode the story it tells.

Selective Color

Color is another area that often gets forgotten. Many Internet entrepreneurs pay little or no attention to color imaging and it's really unfortunate as it is often an inexpensive but effective way of making a profound impression.

Different colors have different psychological effects depending on the context in which they are used. In addition to the color choice, using color as a consistent

Shadow Play
Engagement Technique 16

Shadow Play is a fun technique that stops an audience in its tracks so they can take a second look. When done right, Shadow Play can create the incongruity that demands attention and mental resolution.

The clever implementation of this visual engagement technique can not only deliver the intended message, it can also establish the brand as cutting edge, and in this tech-savvy, consumer-ad-savant era, that's just how you want to be seen.

marketing communication element helps enhance and embed your identity and brand image. If you're not controlling the color in your images then you're missing a great opportunity to make a memorable impression. Of course lack of color (black and white photography) can be just as powerful if used properly.

Another effective implementation of selective color is a B&W photograph that has been adjusted so that part of it is in color. For example, a clothing designer might want a black and white photograph of a model but with the dress she's wearing in color so that the garment stands out and not the model.

Illustrated Photos

Combining a photograph with a drawing can be a very effective way to make a unique impression on your website visitors. British film director Alfred Hitchcock used a similar technique for the introduction to his 1950's television show, where he'd walk on set to lineup with a simple background drawing of his unique and readily recognizable profile. It is a classic example of the Caricature Effect that combines an actual caricature with a photo thereby creating a clever signature style. The image of Hitchcock lining up with his caricature outline is an enduring image of the director that is still recognized more than a half a century later.

Gestalt

By using the Gestalt design concepts of closure, continuance, similarity, proximity, and alignment, you can create a kinetic thought-provoking brand image that demands a second look. Meaning is derived from putting all the pieces together to form a pattern or conclusion.

Focus

Focus is another technique that adds interest and intrigue to an image. In some sense the concept of focus is the essence of marketing. The ability to cognitively lead an audience where you want them to go is exactly what your marketing communication is intended to do.

Augmented Reality

The Internet and digital media changed everything, and I do mean everything. Not only has it opened the door to sophisticated marketing techniques to everyone, it has grown to embrace traditional non-multimedia venues. QR codes and augmented reality videos can now be seen in print magazines, newspapers, direct mail post cards, and window display posters. It's a whole new marketing world filled with possibilities. That said, the technologies by themselves mean nothing unless they are implemented in a 'double take' take-a-second-look manner that demands attention and motivates action.

Cognitive Itch

Even the most well thought-out marketing initiative can fail if it's not implemented properly; and the three elements of cognitive itch (simplicity, repetition, and incongruity) provide direction for how to implement a strategy effectively. At the heart of cognitive itch is the power of sound.

With multimedia now available everywhere and anywhere including print, through augmented reality technologies, it's important to start understanding sound design and the influence it can have on marketing success. All to often sound is relegated to an after-thought when in reality it can both save and enhance an otherwise weak presentation.

Surreal

Much of what has been discussed boils down to a "be bold" approach to delivering your brand story. Incorporating a mind-bending surreal visual identity into your arsenal of marketing weapons can make a impression that will demand attention and of course create that critical second look.

Shadow Plays

This cool technique plays with your audience's brain and demands that double take second look. Have a model or actor strike a pose but have the shadow of the pose display something different. Done right this technique can be very effective.

It's The Differences That People Remember

These examples are only a few of the ways entrepreneurs can create a double-take second look experience: advertising that enhances identity and embeds brand personality in the minds of the audience. Whether it's a display ad, video, website, or packaging design, the thing to keep in mind is that it's the differences that people remember.

In the end it's all about getting your message across, and if your marketing doesn't inspire a second look, a double take, a "I better look at that again" reaction, then it's not marketing, it's noise.

Surreal
Engagement Technique 17

By now you've probably noticed a theme: in order to get people to take a second look, you have to create some kind of incongruity that demands the viewer's attention. Surreal artists like Salvador Dali knew how to create images that pushed reality to its bizarre limits. Melting alarm clocks and weird combinations of elements force viewers to resolve the distorted constructs. The Magritte style bowler hat that keeps popping up in all the Big Idea e-books pays homage to the importance of this visual engagement technique.

Concept 15

Does Creativity Matter (In Business)?

Creativity is like the weather; everyone talks about it but no one does anything about it. Boardrooms, seminars, and conferences are full of talk of the need for creative thinking as a way to spark innovation, new product development, and of course sales, but the sad truth is business leaders for the most part are creatively stunted. Creativity cannot exist in a climate of restrictive rules, tight budgets, and an obsession with technical solutions to human problems.

I can still remember a well-known owner of a major bird food company who was asked if he collected art; he responded by asking the interviewer, why would anyone buy art when they could buy a bird? In general, there seems to be two types of executives, those who see the world through the prism of their product or service with everything else irrelevant or besides the point, and those who could care less what they sell as long as the numbers result in maximized profits.

There are the mavericks like Steve Jobs who ignore the focus groups, spread sheets, and pseudo trends foisted on an ill-informed business community by desperate media outlets too lazy to deliver and explain real news and information: a business sector that has long since lost its way, along with its integrity and pride.

GIF Animation
Engagement Technique 18

Video is the best way to deliver a marketing message because it offers sights, sounds, and motion all in one package; but sometimes, like in an email, video isn't the right choice; and still images just don't deliver the desired impact. In that case, GIF Animations can be the solution. GIF Animations are a series of still images that move. They can be used as part of an email, and receiving an email that opens with a moving image can be the one thing that gets you a better click-through response.

Note: Blurb does not accept GIF Animation files so I have created an MP4 that simulates the effect for e-book purchasers; unfortunately print book owners are stuck with a still image.

People Are Irrational Beings

Business leaders are trained to think rationally and responsibly by adhering to a set of financial criteria, a point-of-view that no reasonable person would argue against. But in a high tech environment filled with new communication venues, the impact of which few people fully understand, owner managers become susceptible to the deluge of hype promoting the latest pop culture fad, supported by statistical manipulations offered-up by those willing to profit from sophisticatedly-challenged business neophytes. What the business community has lost is the core understanding that all business is about people and people are irrational beings governed not by logic but by primitive hardwired instinct.

People are complex, frustrating, and generally an expensive pain-in-the-ass to deal with, so it's no wonder business seeks comfort in bean-counters and application-geeks that promise technical solutions to human problems. Unfortunately that approach is no better than reading tealeaves.

What's The Big Idea?

In the end, every successful company needs to have a Big Idea; without one you are just another also-ran chasing an imaginary pot-of-gold. And since the vast majority of businesses sell a product or service that is substantially the same as hundreds, if not thousands of other companies, why would anyone buy from you. You may be able to survive on convenience or price-cutting but those tactics cannot be sustained in the long-term by most small businesses.

The Parallax Effect
Engagement Technique 19

If you're a fan of PBS you're probably familiar with documentary filmmaker Ken Burns who has made many great films including histories of the Civil War, Jazz, and Baseball. Because Burns goes deep into the archives for old pre-motion picture photographs, he had to find a way to present still images in a television presentation that didn't appear overwhelmingly static. To create more interest he developed a technique, commonly referred to as the Ken Burns technique, that separates the elements of a still image, that are put into 3D space, so that a digitally simulated camera can pan and zoom to create visual interest and the desired second look. If you've purchased the print edition you can access the video on our YouTube channel (http://youtu.be/i6kGS3UPPXo) .

Small business has a tendency to try and emulate their big brother multinationals, but that too is a mistake. Who says big business is efficient let alone creative; not anyone who has ever had to deal with the phone or cable company, or the service department of just about any big business.

Big companies have big budgets, and can do things and experiment with questionable marketing tactics and venues, and when all else fails they can either dominate or buy it in order to control it. So were does that leave you?

Small business needs to be smarter, it needs to use creativity to develop a Big Idea that can be sustained and promoted, one that will make your cupcake, software, or fashion accessory, one that taps into the basic primitive instincts that govern the behavior of each and every person on this planet.

Creativity Ain't Easy

Being in the business of finding creative ways to present our clients' messages is not easy and it's not as arbitrary as it may appear when presented on television or in the media. Being creative for a business client who has all the constrictions, constraints, and budgetary conflicts that limit their own creative thinking is not the same as the creative process of a painter who is basically free to use his or her talent in whatever way and in whatever direction they want.

Business clients must have confidence in the creative contractors they hire or they will sabotage the strategy themselves upon implementation. Big Ideas not only need bold creative thinking in their development, they demand bold

**Cinegraph
Engagement Technique 20**

Whereas the Parallax Effect creates interest by making still images move, the Cinegraph creates it by making moving images still, well almost. The concept is different but the same in that each technique creates an incongruity. To create a Cinegraph you have to mask out everything in a movie that you do not want to move and replace it with a still frame from the same movie. The result can be quite startling when used subtly and in the right context. By now you should be getting the message that incongruity is the key to getting people to take a second look. Note: Blurb doesn't accept GIF Animations and Cinegraphs are GIFs, so I've created a MOV simulation for the e-book; print users are stuck with a still image.

implementation. Many great ideas fail not because the ideas were wrong or flawed but because the client got scared at the last moment and decided to play it safe, or they were unwilling to be patient and wait for the process and strategy to work. Big Ideas require bold implementation, and if you are not prepared to go the whole way, you might as well stick to your same-old-same-old, and limp your way to mediocrity or worse. One of the reasons businesses do not boldly implement Big Ideas is that they do not have confidence in the process their hired marketing hands have used to create it, and instead rely on the tech and stats to provide creative answers to human psychological questions.

These lessons have all been learned before, but like much of history the answers get buried under the weight of pop-culture profiteering that masquerades as progress. The reality is businesses need to think creatively, but don't. Ergo a solution is required, and its not good enough for marketing agencies to just say they're creative, they must convince clients that creativity answers the question: "what the hell do people really want?"

That's Nice, But What About The Science?

It is easy to pooh-pooh creativity and storytelling as leisure irrelevancies but Eric Kandel, a Nobel Prize winning neuropsychiatrist and author of "The Age of Insight: The Quest to Understand the Unconscious on Art, Mind and Brain" writes, art and storytelling, "are low-risk, imaginative ways of solving problems." Art focuses attention, removes distraction, and engages the brain through metaphorical representation. Art is a mnemonic device that points us in the right direction by representing universal truths.

Our strongest instinct is to survive both physiologically and emotionally. Art and storytelling helps us workout problem situations, both critical and mundane, by delivering a vicarious experience that informs, enlightens, and educates without the pain and consequences of learning by first hand experience. Are creativity, art, and storytelling important to business? You bet they are.

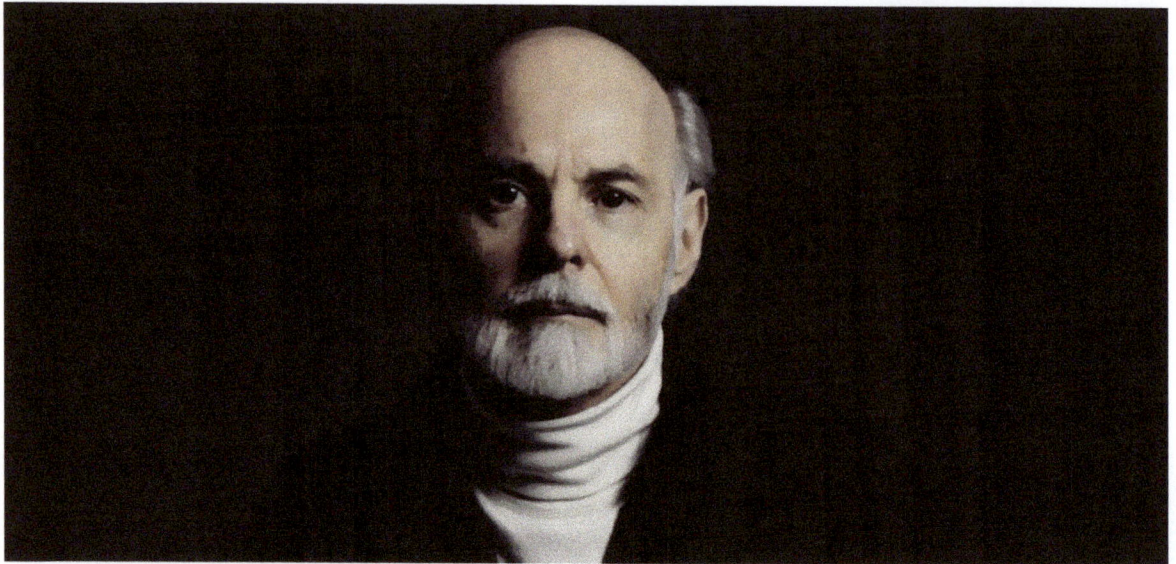

WHAT'S THE BIG IDEA?

Jerry Bader is Senior Partner at MRPwebmedia (www.
mrpwebmedia.com) a marketing and design firm that
specializes in creating video campaigns for clients. "Double
Take" is the third in a series of marketing e-books designed to
help entrepeneurs develop effective marketing startegies.

MRPwebmedia provides a turnkey solution from concept to
post production including everything from idea generation
and script writing to special effects and custom music and
sound design.

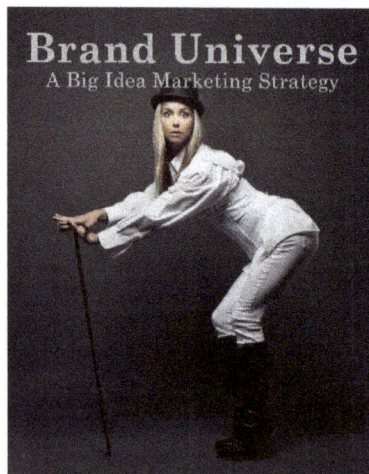

Other books by Jerry Bader

Brand Universe
A Big Idea Marketing Strategy
http://store.blurb.com/ebooks/p8b3ac01f0cabebf4d1e8 (http:
//store.blurb.com/ebooks/p8b3ac01f0cabebf4d1e8)

What's The Big Idea?
A Guide To Creative Marketing Communication
http://store.blurb.com/ebooks/408096-what-s-the-big-idea
(http://store.blurb.com/ebooks/408096-what-s-the-big-idea)

www.ingramcontent.com/pod-product-compliance
Lightning Source LLC
Chambersburg PA
CBHW051311020426
42333CB00027B/3302